# Switching Lanes

## A Road Map to Balance and Joy

### Vikki Carrel

Copyright © 2004 Vikki Carrel

Published by MMI Press

*All rights reserved.* No part of this book may be reproduced or transmitted in any form or by any means, electronic or mechanical, including photocopying, recording or by any information storage and retrieval system, without permission in writing from the publisher, except by a reviewer, who may quote brief passages in a review.

Editing by Janis Wilkins-Mash
Book Design by The Printed Page
Cover Design by Julie Macon Hill
Author Photo by Art Bromwell

Printed in the United States of America.

ISBN 0-9761861-0-1

# *Dedication*

To my husband, Jeff
and our sons, Corbett and Cason …
there is joy in my journey because
you travel the road with me.

*Switching Lanes*

> *It is always better to work on who you want to be as opposed to what you want to do or how you want to look. When you have clarity about the kind of person you want to be, you are driven to fulfill that vision.*
>
> —Oprah Winfrey

*Switching Lanes*

# Contents

Introduction . . . . . . . . . . . . . . . . . . . . . . . . . . . 1

Chapter 1. The Balancing Act . . . . . . . . . . . . . . . . . 7
   Imbalance vs. Balance. . . . . . . . . . . . . . . . . . . . 9
   My Joy Circle . . . . . . . . . . . . . . . . . . . . . . . 10
   The Joy Circle Questionnaire . . . . . . . . . . . . . . . 13
   My Joy Circle Adjustments . . . . . . . . . . . . . . . . 20
   The Principles of Balance . . . . . . . . . . . . . . . . 21
   Attitude. . . . . . . . . . . . . . . . . . . . . . . . . . . 23
   Sticky-Note Theory . . . . . . . . . . . . . . . . . . . . 25

Chapter 2. Don't Postpone Joy . . . . . . . . . . . . . . . . 29
   Action Plan for Joy. . . . . . . . . . . . . . . . . . . . . 35

Chapter 3. Drive over Your Limitations . . . . . . . . . . . 41

Chapter 4. You Don't Need to Rehearse to Be Yourself . . . . 53
   The Value Structure Chart . . . . . . . . . . . . . . . . 55

Chapter 5. The Game of Life . . . . . . . . . . . . . . . . . 63
   Self Inventory Exercise . . . . . . . . . . . . . . . . . . 65

Chapter 6. Recharge Your Life . . . . . . . . . . . . . . . . 73

Chapter 7. Switching Lanes . . . . . . . . . . . . . . . . . 81

*If you think you can, you can.
And if you think you can't,
you're right.*

—Mary Kay Ash

# *Acknowledgments*

> *I would maintain that thanks
> are the highest form of thought,
> and that gratitude is happiness
> doubled by wonder.*
> —Gilbert Keith Chesterton

Writing this book has been a journey I will never forget, one that has involved the support and inspiration of my wonderful family and friends.

It is with love and deep gratitude that I thank my loving husband Jeff for making my dreams come true and this project possible. His encouragement and willingness to believe in me has made all the difference. Our sons, Corbett and Cason, are the reason I wrote this book. They have unlocked the joys within me that come from the gift of motherhood. Their love and laughter inspire me each day.

It is with humility that I acknowledge my extraordinary parents, Donna and Dick Pack, who have taught me unconditional love. Their examples and endless sacrifices are a great blessing in my life. My sisters, Cathy Goodrich and Debra Collett are my best friends and their enduring support and friendship are gifts I treasure.

I wish to express my appreciation and sincere thanks to Janis Wilkins-Mash, my writing coach for editing the manuscript; Lisa Liddy, for designing the book; and Julie Hill, for the cover design. Their patience, talent and dedication to this project has been invaluable.

I would like to honor my dear friends and past business partners, Debbi Webb and the late Sherry Grimes. Thanks to Debbi, for teaching me to listen to my inner voice and to dream big and to Sherry, for teaching me to believe in myself and my abilities as a motivational speaker.

I wish to pay tribute to the people who freely gave of their time, hearts and resources to support me and this project. A partial list includes those special friends who reviewed my manuscript, Shelley Ashby, Rebecca Ortiz, Vera Resch, Deb Zuech-Smyrl, Lynn Schoendorfer, Anne Martin, Beth Meise, Amy Roper, Lisa Wood, and to the many others for their cheers of encouragement along the way.

# Introduction

> *I am not afraid of storms*
> *for I am learing how to*
> *sail my own ship.*
> —Louisa May Alcott

This book began as a project with my business partner Sherry to co-author a book based on the information from our motivational seminars. Following these seminars we often received requests from our audience for audio tapes or books they could purchase. What began as a simple project to meet their requests has ended up a life changing experience for me. The road I traveled when I began writing this book is very different than the road I travel today.

In my high school yearbook my close friend Lisa wrote the following entry: "Know in my heart there is a special place called VIKKI. The writer Roy Croft says it better than I can when he wrote...I love you not only for what you are but for what I am when I am with you. Vikki that is the greatest gift of all gifts....*Goodness*. You are continually a good influence on me...and for that I will always be grateful." As I reflect over my past I recognize that I have been blessed with many special people in my life like Lisa. Individuals who acknowledged in me long before I did, that I had gifts and talents to share, one being the ability to influence others for good.

This process of recognizing gifts and talents in myself has not been easy. Growing up my alias was *the girl with a plan B*. I became a pro at taking lemons and turning them into lemonade. The reason I became so good at this process was because life handed me many lemons. If you were to chat with my high school classmates you would learn that I wasn't the most beautiful, talented or popular girl in my graduating class. I ran for school office eight times and lost each election before I finally won. I tried out for the school's concert choir, musical and the prestigious cheerleading squad only to be told that I didn't have the talent to become a member. Through all of these disappointments I learned in my youth the importance of *try, try, again*. This motto continues to sustain me as an adult.

The roads we choose to travel are not always the scenic routes with beautiful, awe inspiring landscapes. For me I have spent much of my time traveling down roads that required road maps and traffic signs to get me from point A to point B. At times I felt lost, confused and disappointed in myself. I learned along the way that talent is part of the equation to achieve success and that hard work and determination make up the other part. What I lack in talent I've made up in determination and hard work. Life is a learning process and each day I continue to learn. I have conquered some of my fears and have others yet to face. Writing this book was often times a frightening, difficult and frustrating experience for me. I was fortunate to have talented people join me in this journey and because of their dedication to this project, friendships developed and the process of writing this book became a life altering experience for me.

For you, the reader, my hope is that this book will encourage you to embrace each day, to recognize your self worth, to motivate you to overcome your limitations and to inspire you to balance your life and to find inner peace. Enjoy your journey wherever it may take you and don't forget to turn lemons into lemonade.

*Switching Lanes*

*Action may not always bring happiness; but there is no happiness without action.*

—Benjamin Disraeli

*Switching Lanes*

## Chapter 1

# The Balancing Act

I loved going to the circus as a child and even now as an adult with my own children. The sight of various animals such as lions, tigers, elephants and bears dancing around the center ring, the funny clowns and high wire acts were all exciting to watch. It was breath taking to see the performers walk across a thin wire high above the crowd carrying chairs and umbrellas without losing their balance. Their balancing acts still continue to amaze me as an adult. Like those high wire performers, I find the ability to balance one's life in today's world just as intense and intriguing. Today many of us must develop similar types of courage, determination and inner strength to stay balanced on our own high wire of everyday living.

If you were to stand on one leg while balancing the other above the ground, you quickly realize that staying balanced is difficult. After a few moments on one leg, you begin to wobble trying to grab for something to hold on to. Is that how you feel at times during a hectic day, like you are balancing on one leg ready to topple over? In order to give balance to a wobbling body standing on one leg, the simplest solution is to set your other foot on the ground. Moving from the instability of one leg to the stability of two legs required action, even if it was a minimal one. Once you are standing on two legs balanced, stability returns. Therefore balance can be defined as that which gives equilibrium, or the condition of feeling stable. Balancing your life begins with YOU taking action. If you choose not to take action, the consequences could result in an imbalanced life. It is taking action that moves your life from instability to stability.

Let's consider what an imbalanced life has to offer. The result of an imbalanced life could bring about negative feelings such as chaos, disharmony and stress. These negative feelings then can impact your direction and control of your daily routine. Chaos, disharmony and stress will move you away from feelings of joy and inner peace. To rid yourself of these negative feelings in your life, the first step is to identify what interferes with obtaining balance in your life.

Think of your life as a large circle divided into three sections. The first section is your *associations*, comprised of your emotional relationships with yourself, your spiritual self and others around you such as family, friends and co-workers. The second section is your *activities*. This section encompasses what you do during a given day. It is your schedule, your physical relationship involving family, friends, work, church, community involvement, and so on. The third section includes your *assets*. Included in this section are items that are sentimental and of little monetary value up to high priced items of greater value. Together, these three sections when balanced create your **Joy Circle**, or the joy you feel in life. Joy comes from stability between the three sections. Chaos, disharmony and stress will result when one of these sections is larger, thus dominating one or both of the other two sections, resulting in a **Joy Circle** that is out of balance.

## *Imbalance vs. Balance*

**Chaos = Imbalance**  **Joy = Balance**

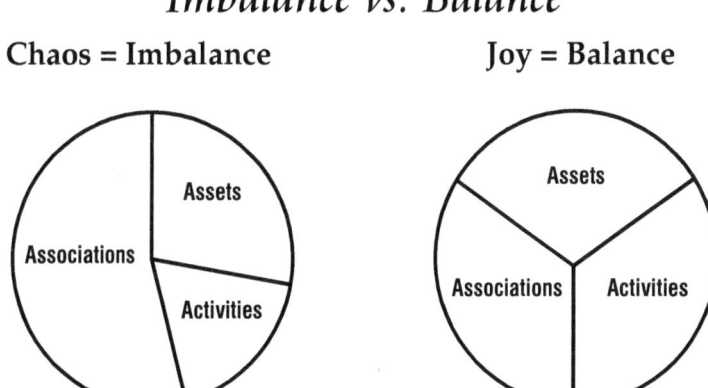

As a fashion show choreographer, my schedule was extremely hectic. I worked long hours, six to seven days a week, for extended periods of time, producing fashion events. My life was out of balance and as a result I felt limited joy. The result of my choice to maintain a hectic schedule caused me to feel tremendous stress and my health began to suffer. Although I loved my job, I had no time to enjoy life. I was so busy establishing a solid reputation and economic base that there was little time to make a life. The *activities and assets sections* dominated my **Joy Circle**.

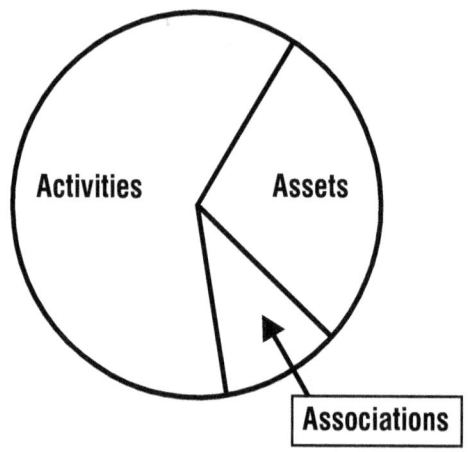

## My Joy Circle
(as a fashion show choreographer)

I chose to have little time to interact with my family and friends. I was driven by the goal to acquire a solid economic base, in doing so; I allowed no time for pleasure in my life with my husband Jeff and our young son Corbett. The imbalance in my life became very evident to me one day when I over heard my son calling our full time nanny, Sara, 'Mommy'. That was a startling reality check for me and at that moment I realized it was time for me to rearrange my priorities. In order to bring balance to my **Joy Circle**, I needed to take action and implement change. I knew leaving my job as a fashion show choreographer would allow me to gain control over how I spent my time. I was responsible for a staff of 100 plus people; therefore, managing this group is what was really controlling my schedule. Once I identified the source of imbalance in my life, I began to implement change. One step at a time was the method that worked for me. First, I quit working. The approach I took was the cold turkey approach; I left the fashion industry and quit producing fashion shows. This is the option that worked for me. Not everyone will choose this approach.

Next, I spent several months trying to redefine myself. For fifteen years I had seen myself as a fashion show choreographer. My family and friends had known me as a professional who was always on the run with late night rehearsals and early morning meetings. In a nutshell, this was my identity. When I stopped working I realized there was a need to establish new goals and begin making changes in my lifestyle. I began by altering my daily routine and learning how to slow down, which forced me to step outside of my comfort zone. Making these changes was hard work. I had not realized how much hard work was entailed and the difficulty that change demands. Defining the new me was a real challenge; I was actually in control of my time and my daily schedule, free to enjoy activities of my choosing. At times, I was uncomfortable with the new me I had defined for myself; yet I recognized that these modifications in my life were healthy and necessary for my well being. It is important to remember that change can be STRESSFUL. The level of stress increases when one attempts to change their routine or alter a particular habit. Stress can be a good thing when change occurs in an effort to increase personal feelings of joy and inner peace. The journey of getting there may cause temporary feelings of stress: however, in the long run those feelings of stress are well worth enduring when the final outcome is positive.

A year after I left the fashion industry our second child, Cason, was born. It was amazing to witness how this joyful event sent my schedule into a tail spin. Having two children under the age of five brought a new type of chaos, disharmony and stress into my life. I had exchanged the stresses of producing fashion events for the stresses of motherhood. The happiness that children bring to one's life is greater than life itself but the responsibilities are also challenging. The process of defining the new me and becoming a full time mom, without the help of a nanny, all in one year proved to be overwhelming. To assist me with this evolution of change, I relied on the tool of insight to aid me along in this process of self definition and of learning how to manage the new stresses in my life. The tool that benefited me the most was the mind set of living in the moment. I had often spent time looking towards tomorrow, not embracing the moments and happiness found in each day. The new me, was beginning to understand this new reality.

My final step in this process was to develop a new career that I would enjoy and one that would be compatible with my family responsibilities, which were now my first priority. I found it. Today, I am a motivational speaker. Six years after Cason was born, I began to present motivational seminars. As a motivational speaker I manage my time, my schedule and I have just one employee, myself. A career change is just what I needed, but not everyone will need to make such a drastic change. I discovered that the *one step at a time method* worked for me. In the beginning, I tried to overhaul several areas of my life all at once, however, that approach caused me to feel overwhelmed. Then I tried focusing on one change in my routine at a time that was manageable for me. This process allowed me to experience success one change at a time.

Finding joy and inner peace, requires that you take a closer look at the balance of each section within your own **Joy Circle**. Begin to examine for yourself the relationships in and between your associations, assets and activities. The following questionnaire will help you begin to access sections of your **Joy Circle** to determine if your circle is balanced or imbalanced.

## *The Joy Circle Questionnaire*

In the first section, answer questions about your Associations with yourself and others. Based on your answers to these questions on Associations, assign a value between 0 – 360.

**0 value** would represent no joy being derived from Associations in your **Joy Circle**.

**360 value** would represent that total joy is derived from Associations in your **Joy Circle**.

You will also be establishing a value for the Assets and Activities portions of your **Joy Circle**. Total value for all three sections must equal 360.

## I. Associations

### A. Myself

1. Do I schedule time in each day for myself?

2. Each day I spend time for myself doing the following...

3. I would like to schedule time in my schedule for myself doing the following....

### B. Others

1. Who are my associates that influence me and why?

    A. positively

    B. negatively

2. Do the individuals that I spend time with uplift me and help me to be a better person?

   A. List three ways you are influenced in a positive way.

   1.

   2.

   3.

   B. List three ways you are influenced in a negative way.

   1.

   2.

   3.

**C. Spirituality**

1. Is spiritual involvement important to me?

If yes, why?


If no, why?


Association Rating:_____

## II. Assets

In the second section, answer questions about your assets and possessions.

1. Do I spend too much time worrying about material possessions? Why?



2. Do money and material objects determine my joy and self worth? Explain.



3. Do I find joy through sharing my possessions with others?

   If yes, why?

   If not, why?


Based upon your answers to the above questions on Assets, assign the value that Assets represent in your Joy Circle.

Assets Rating:_____

## III. Activities

In the third section, answer questions about your activities and schedule.

1. Do I control my activities or do they control me? Explain.

2. Do I allow others to over-schedule my time? Explain.

3. Do I try to accomplish too many activities in one day? Explain.

Based upon your answers to the above questions on Activities, assign the value that Activities represent in your Joy Circle.

Activities Rating:_____

## IV. Divide Your Joy Circle

Divide your **Joy Circle** into three sections based on the values given for each section. Label the sections as Associations, Assets and Activities.

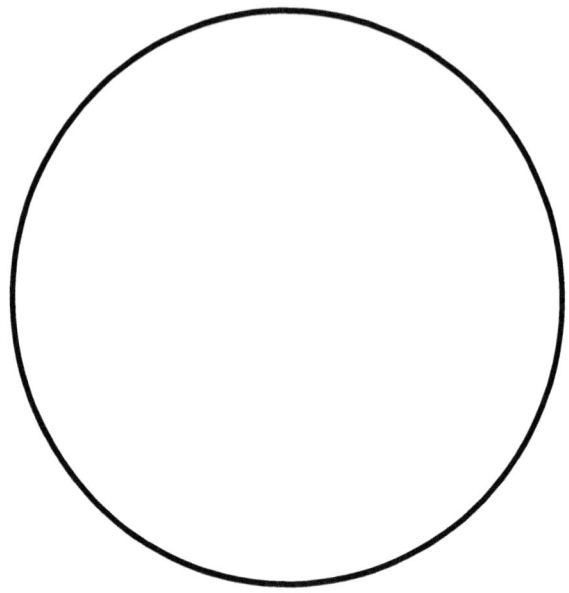

After completing your **Joy Circle** examine the three sections. Are the three sections of the circle balanced or does one section control the other sections of your **Joy Circle**? If one or two sections dominate your **Joy Circle**, adjustments need to be made in order for you to feel balance in your life. Joy and inner peace are achieved when the sections within your **Joy Circle** are in balance with each other. It is important to remember that your **Joy Circle** may never be perfectly balanced.

This exercise is to help you identify stress factors and extreme imbalances in your life. Look at your **Joy Circle** and determine what adjustments need to be made to bring balance to your **Joy Circle** and most important, how you will do it. To complete this exercise it is necessary to make adjustments. For example, let's suppose that you are an impulsive buyer, spending money that you do not have in your monthly budget. This would cause the **Assets** section of your **Joy Circle** to dominate the other two sections, causing your **Joy Circle** to be out of balance. An adjustment would be necessary in order to bring balance to your **Joy Circle**. You may decide to adjust the **Assets** section by using cash, not checks or credit cards for your purchases thus preventing you from spending too much money.

Another solution might be to make a list of items to be purchased from the store, before you go. As you shop rely on that list, not deviating from it, preventing you from purchasing unnecessary items. You will probably try many options as you fine-tune the areas in your life that are holding you back from feeling joy. Write down the changes you will make in your life to help you feel more joy. These adjustments may take a week, a month or even a year to achieve the balance that is right for you. Take a close look at the balance within your **Joy Circle** and refer to the Joy Circle Questionnaire as needed. Even if the sections of your circle may never be divided into equal parts, balance is something you can achieve. The following is a practical activity.

## My Joy Circle Adjustments

In order to feel more balance and joy in my life, I will work on adjusting the following section of my **Joy Circle**. (Underline one)

**Associations**     **Assets**     **Activities**

I will implement three adjustments in that section of my **Joy Circle**. First, identify the adjustment. Second, identify the action to be taken in order to make the adjustment.

1. Adjustment:

Action to be taken:


2. Adjustment:

Action to be taken:


3. Adjustment:

Action to be taken:

After identifying the adjustments that need to be made within your **Joy Circle**, begin to take action and implement change. The process to implement adjustments may come easily for you or it may not. If you find it difficult to move forward with the action and to make change, The Principles of Balance may be helpful to you.

## *The Principles of Balance*

During the time I spent producing fashion shows, I coordinated hundreds of outfits to be worn by runway models. I learned early on that in order for an outfit to have flair it had to have *balance*. The balance for each outfit on the runway was the key to the success of a style show. Balance for an outfit is achieved by **line, texture, color** and **accessory**. These same four principles can also be applied to balancing one's life.

**Line** in the fashion industry is a basic fashion principle. Line gives direction to an outfit resulting in a fashion silhouette. Feeling balance in your life can be obtained in the same way, it helps you define who you are. When coordinating an outfit the favorable line is for the model to appear tall and thin. This is accomplished when there is a harmonious relationship between the pieces of clothing that make up the outfit and the model's physical proportions. Line gives direction to the pieces in the outfit, resulting in balanced proportions. Ask yourself, is the direction of my life moving in balance with how I define myself? Determine what is important to you and in what order.

Identify the terms you want to live by and prioritize them. When you are moving in a direction that is in balance with how you define yourself, joy can be achieved and inner peace felt.

Experts on fabric describe texture as the feel of the fabric. A fabric's **texture** affects the way you feel when you wear the fabric. Likewise the way you feel certainly impacts the balance in your life. The texture of the fabric is determined by the fiber content and the weave of the yarn. A silk blouse feels very differently than a knobby wool jacket. The texture of a fabric can affect your mood while wearing it. Texture provides the emotional components for an outfit. When you deal with texture it is important to be extremely conscious of it. Texture is much like the emotional components of your life. When you deal with your emotions it is also important to be extremely conscious of them. In order to balance your life you need to understand your emotions. Learn to manage your emotions. Be quick to recognize your emotional limitations. On days when you feel emotionally sensitive make adjustments to your schedule. Recognize your limitations at home and in the work place. Remember, you cannot be everything to everyone. Take control of your time and learn to manage your schedule.

**Color** according to Stephen Burrows, a noted fashion designer "All colors go—it's just a matter of how you put them together. Colors should be happy—like toys." Just like the multiplicity of color, the multiplicity of one's behavior is attitude. Attitude contributes to balance or imbalance in your life. Color creates a mood and produces a strong initial impression. The color red is bold and powerful, while pastels are soft and pleasing. Fashion designer, Fernando Sanchez, sums up color perfectly; "One's clothes should be in accordance with one's attitudes, and the colors in accordance with one's personality." Color creates an attitude for clothing. Song writers use color to help define certain attitudes. The color emphasis also works effectively in songs. For example, the song "It's *Not Easy Being Green*", sung by Sesame Street's Kermit the Frog and the theme song from the movie, "*Lady Sings the Blues*", sung by Diana Ross, provides attitude in music. Color also projects attitude in clothing. In balancing your life, think of color as essential as attitude. I agree with what author, Charles Swindoll has written about attitude, his treatise will help you to recognize that you have tremendous control over how you react to your circumstances, through your attitude.

## *Attitude*

*"The longer I live, the more I realize the impact of attitude on life. Attitude, to me, is more important than facts. It is more important than the past, than education, than money, than circumstances, than failures, than successes, than what other people think or say or do. It is more important than appearance, giftedness or skill. It will make or break a company… a church… a home. The remarkable thing is we have a choice every day regarding the attitude we will embrace for that day. We cannot change the inevitable. The only thing we can do is play on the one string we have, and that is our*

*attitude... I am convinced that life is 10% what happens to me, and 90% how I react to it. And so it is with you... we are in charge of our Attitudes."*

The fourth principle, **accessory** is crucial in the fashion industry and a balanced life. Accessories shape and define an outfit and can renew last season's dated sweater or blazer. The right accessory adds the finishing touches to the balance of an outfit. Accessories are divided into two categories, essentials and extras. The essential accessories are stockings, shoes and a handbag. These accessories are necessary to complete the outfit. The extra accessories are those items such as a scarf, hat or jewelry. These accessory items add style and jazz up an outfit. The extra accessories make dressing unique, individualized, creative and fun.

You must learn to prioritize the essentials and extras in your life and learn to not over accessorize. Therefore, using the **Joy Circle** will help you determine which accessories in your life are essentials or extras. The essentials in your life are yourself, family, job, and place of worship. The extras or non-essentials in your life could be the bowling league, the pottery class, community involvement, etc. When you begin to feel stressed and over-scheduled take a close look at the extras in your life, you may need to scale back. Allow accessories to teach you how to balance and define your life. If you are wearing too many accessories remove a few of the 'extras' and you will be amazed how you begin to feel more balance in your life. The principles of the fashion industry may be just what you need to help keep balance in your life.

Chapter 1 The Balancing Act

Fashion is fascinating and is a vital part of our everyday lives. The longer I worked in the fashion industry, the more aware I became of the impact and influence fashion had on my daily existence. Makeup expert, Way Bandy, may be the one who said it best, "People who have style have a strong self image and a positive self-esteem - a strong sense of being."

The balancing act in one's life is achievable with line, texture, color and accessory, so let the principles of fashion become your guide to joy.

## *Sticky-Note Theory*

**An additional concept that you might find helpful in the process of balancing your life is the Sticky Note Theory.** Imagine that all the input you receive each day comes in the form of those original yellow sticky notes. Visualize yourself at the end of the day with sticky notes attached all over your body, from the top of your head to bottom of your feet. It is your responsibility to remove the sticky notes containing negative information. Don't get bogged down in unhealthy comments that do not benefit you, but keep the positive messages and super glue them to yourself. This will insure that the direction you are moving into is balanced with who you are.

Refer back to your **Joy Circle** from time to time to keep maintaining balance between your associations, assets and activities. In order to maintain balance in your life you may need to gather additional information from other sources such as magazine articles, books, by attending seminars or seeking out professional help. Ultimately, it is up to you to define your **Joy Circle** and obtain inner peace.

*Learning to live in the
present moment is part
of the path of joy.*
—Sarah Ban Breathnach

*Switching Lanes*

*Chapter 2*

# Don't Postpone Joy

A few years ago I was driving down the freeway aware of very little other than the traffic on all sides of me. I noticed one of the bumper stickers on the car in front of me. It read, **Don't Postpone Joy.** This prompted me to think about whether or not I had postponed joy in my own life. For several more miles I wondered why it is that some people seem to have continuous joy in their lives while others spend a lifetime trying to find it. I decided to take a closer look at the similarities and differences between the feeling of Joy and Happiness.

Oprah Winfrey, the well known TV Host said, "You feel real joy in direct proportion to how you are living your truth." For me, joy is the sustained inner peace you feel when you find balance while moving your life in a positive direction. This positive direction is set in motion when your self definition is in balance with the direction your life is moving. Happiness is the feeling of pleasure that results from good fortune or an event. Most often, however happiness is NOT sustained for a long period of time. Therefore, the major difference between Happiness and Joy is simply that Happiness is temporary but Joy is not.

Joy is available for everyone. You will find out that change is often required in your daily routine and the way you think, in order to increase the joy in your life. You are required to determine the amount of joy you want in your life. For many of us, life is like a roller coaster ride. It has high peaks, low valleys, sudden turns, twisty jerks and quick abrupt stops. You must arrange your life so joy will be probable. Joy is available for everyone regardless of their personal circumstances. Just as one adjusts to the coaster ride, you also determine the joy you feel.

One unfortunate example of Joy verses Happiness is demonstrated in the circumstances of my good friend who was in a physically and emotionally abusive marriage. Her life became so difficult and unbearable that she filed for divorce and moved with her children from their home into a small apartment. She feared for herself and her children's safety. During the next six months, I observed her lifestyle. She felt limited joy in her life during this time yet she was capable of feeling happiness. Why? Joy was postponed in her life because her self definition and the direction of her life were not in balance. She only relished moments of happiness because of her children. She did not feel any joy during this time, but did obtain moments of happiness. Her happiness came when her children excelled in school and in athletic activities.

It can probably be asserted that mastering joy is a state of being, subsequently, joy begins with you. You must plan for joy in your life. Therefore, you need to arrange your life so that there will be more joy. Cason, our youngest son, is an expert at arranging his life so joy is likely. He embraces each day with zest and zeal realizing that life has much to offer him. Most children's approach to life is simple and honest, they live in the moment, recognizing each day as a new beginning. As you begin to evaluate what is preventing you from feeling joy in your life, allow children to be your teacher and simplify your approach to mastering joy.

The first step towards the feeling of joy is to minimize the stress in your life. Begin by identifying what is causing you to feel stressed. You must identify the stress first and then find ways to eliminate or reduce that stress. Lack of joy is the result of many physical and emotional conditions such as mental strain, physical pain or an emotional breakdown, these can be results of a stress-filled lifestyle.

Let's take a look at three ways to reduce stress and obtain joy.

    1) Improve time management
    2) Resolve unresolved conflicts
    3) Define personal limitations

To improve time management, first, don't over-schedule your time. Be realistic about what you can accomplish in a day. By setting unrealistic goals regarding your time you set yourself up for failure. Learn to say NO, you can not be everything for everyone. An effective tool that works for many people that might help you is to make a to do list. Make a list of what needs to be accomplished in a given day. Then prioritize that list from the most important to the least important. It is more effective to set your list with fewer items, providing yourself with a realistic list rather than one of unrealistic tasks. Life with limited frustrations cuts down on one's stress level, making it the first step towards helping you feel inner freedom and joy.

Next, don't allow unresolved conflict to prevent you from feeling joy. Unresolved conflict is the result of a situation in your life that did not receive final closure. For example, an unpaid parking ticket may cost hundreds of dollars when left unpaid. If you have unsettled business with yourself, a family member or friends, settle it. You need to evaluate your personal situation and decide if emotional closure will do the trick or if physical closure needs to take place.

The best way to resolve conflict within yourself is to let go of all negative feelings that you have towards yourself. Do not allow negative energy to become destructive eroding away at your personal joy and inner peace. If you are not satisfied with how you define yourself, think about what changes will help. In order to resolve personal conflict it could be necessary to review your goals and values that involve family, career and self. Goals change as the phases of your life change and they need to be reviewed and adjusted over time.

A period in my own mother's life illustrates the benefits of goal adjustments. Mother had taught school for twenty years or so and felt the desire to do some additional post graduate work. These additional hours would increase her retirement pay. Soon after she began her studies her mother became very ill with Leukemia. At this time my mother found it necessary to re-evaluate her goal. She found it difficult to work full-time as an educator, take night classes at the local university, care for her family and help her terminally ill mother. My mother recognized that her goal of furthering her education needed to be delayed for a time. She withdrew from the university program, continued to teach school during the day allowing her the time to care for her family and her terminally ill mother. The next year my mother enrolled in classes to achieve her education goal. Adjusting her goal temporarily allowed her the time she needed to balance family and career.

A good friend of mine shared her experience with me that also illustrated how goals change. Janice spent several years working in corporate America where she achieved success and felt great satisfaction. Over time, she began to feel stress in her life trying to balance a demanding career and a family, leaving her with feelings of inadequacy and very little joy. Janice was struggling with internal conflict. Her original goals to achieve success in her corporate America job were being over-shadowed by her desire to be at home full time raising her two young children. Quite simply, her goals had changed. She quit her job to be at home with her children. An important point to remember—what is right for one person may not be the answer for another. Not everyone will choose to make such a drastic adjustment in their personal goals and direction, Janice did what she felt was right for her and her children. Evaluating and adjusting personal goals may help you to resolve personal conflicts in your life allowing you to more accurately define yourself and therefore feel more joy.

Continuing on the path to find joy can be obtained when emotional closure happens enabling you to let go of negative feelings towards a person or a circumstance. Those who hold onto negative feelings become emotionally unhealthy. You need to evaluate your personal situation and take action towards resolving conflict in your life. Take personal ownership for any wrongdoing you have committed towards another person. Making a phone call or writing a letter to the person you need to resolve conflict with may be necessary. Recognize that you are responsible for your actions towards this final closure and that you cannot control how the other party will react. Professional help may be needed to help resolve conflict with another person.

In order to resolve internal conflict with yourself and external conflict with others, change must occur. Ask yourself, what conflict in my life is holding me back from feeling joy and am I willing to adjust my attitudes and actions? Recognize that you must do several things, 1) let go of negative feelings towards yourself, 2) understand that goals change over time and may need to be adjusted and 3) you must take personal ownership for your attitudes and actions towards yourself and others. Holding onto unresolved conflict is unhealthy and prevents you from feeling inner peace and joy.

Take an inventory of your current situation and life style. What is holding you back from feeling joy? Complete the following **Action Plan for Joy** and begin to eliminate some of your daily stresses. Do not allow your personal limitations, such as a negative attitude or procrastination, to produce stress in your life. A personal inventory will help you recognize your personal limitations and how you can begin to manage those limitations, turning them into your strengths.

## *Action Plan for Joy*

Complete the following questions about yourself being as honest as you can.

1. *What is holding me back from feeling inner peace?*

- 1
- 2
- 3

2. What are my personal limitations?

- 1
- 2
- 3

3. How can I change these limitations and make them my strengths?

- 1
- 2
- 3

4. I see myself eliminating……

- 1
- 2
- 3

5. I see myself becoming…..

- 1
- 2
- 3

After completing the questions, can you identify any stresses that should and can be eliminated? If there are any, what are they?

✳ 1

✳ 2

✳ 3

After evaluating your **Action Plan for Joy**, ask yourself, is it time for me to make change and are the options available for me to make change? Do not allow excuses to become walls, preventing you from moving towards joy in your life. Arranging your life so more joy is possible will require that you make change. Change can be difficult and most people resist change. Refer back to your **Action Plan for Joy.** Do not attempt to overhaul everything in your life all at once. Focus on one thing at a time, moving forward at a pace that is comfortable for you. Some people may choose to start with big changes in their lives while others may begin with smaller ones. In order to feel inner peace you must make changes in your life so joy is more likely to be felt. Examples of those changes might be setting goals, meeting deadlines or rearranging personal priorities. Take the necessary steps to eliminate stress in your life; do not over schedule your time. Second, make your limitations your strengths and finally, try to resolve conflict in your life.

*Switching Lanes*

What can you change in your life today to eliminate stress?

✷ 1

✷ 2

Begin to focus on joy. The sooner you recognize what is preventing you from feeling inner peace and make the necessary changes, the quicker you will begin to feel joy. Therefore, when your definition of yourself is in balance with the direction your life is moving, joy is the sustained feeling of inner peace that comes.

*One can never consent
to creep when one feels
an impulse to soar.*

—Helen Keller

*Switching Lanes*

## Chapter 3

# *Drive over Your Limitations*

'Dress-up' is a childhood activity many young girls enjoy, the wearing of high heeled shoes and draping themselves in over-sized clothing, pretending to be their favorite movie star. The application of make-up is also an important part of the dress-up experience, applying bright colored shadow and lipstick to the eyes and lips. Dressed fashionably from head-to-toe the young girls then parade about strutting their high fashion looks, awaiting applause from those around them. This childhood activity becomes a lifelong ritual for most women, the wearing of fashionable clothing, applying the perfect make-up colors and then anxiously awaiting the finale, the verbal approval from family and friends.

Strutting down a runway as a high fashion model is the grown-up version of the childhood activity of 'dress-up'. Wearing high heeled shoes and being draped in expensive designer clothing is a little girl's dream profession. Working as a fashion show choreographer,

I spent endless hours backstage of extravagant fashion sets. One aspect of the business that always amazed me was the transformation of the appearance of the models. They would walk on to the fashion set looking very plain with their hair pulled straight back in a chignon and little to no make-up on their faces. The make up artists worked their magic, applying foundations and colors to enhance each model's facial features. Within minutes these plain looking women were transformed into beautiful high fashion models, to be admired by audiences around the world. In the world of high fashion, make-up artists are essential to the visual success of a fashion event. It is the job of a make-up artist to camouflage the models' facial imperfections and enhance their positively beautiful features. This same concept can be applied to everyday life, to focus on the positive while learning to overcome the negative.

The fashion business taught me many lessons. One lesson I hold most valuable was learning to overcome limitations. Every fashion show I produced was an original, with a different set of circumstances and resources. The resources varied, ranging from the financial budgets, to the modeling staff, music selections, backdrops and special effects. Each fashion event along with its unique set of circumstances and limitations, forced my business partner, Debbi and I to become resourceful. We learned that no fashion show provided us with unlimited resources.

In the beginning, our fashion production business consisted of bookings for clothing retailers with limited finances for fashion shows. Conservative financial budgets prevented us from using the best models in the industry or extravagant backdrops for the runway scenery. Regardless of the circumstances, the goal for Debbi and I was still the same, to produce a superior fashion show. In order to accomplish our goal we relied on the circumstances within our control. Quality and professionalism were the ingredients our reputation was built upon. If we had waited for perfect conditions, we would have never produced a single fashion event. What a tremendous loss this would have been for us, the models, production staff and the audience of viewers and buyers.

Along the way, we learned that the limitations we could not change or control could become an asset. This challenge caused us to be more creative, resulting in a runway show production style unique to the fashion industry.

Walking away from our limitations prevents us from learning lessons that benefit us and others. Often, our limitations become our strengths.

A great inspiration to me and a wonderful example of this point is our oldest son, Corbett. He has difficulty with written expression. Corbett did not run from this limitation. He hit it head on, making it his strength. When he was in the fifth grade he was a member of his school's student newspaper staff and was selected to represent his school as an author at the Young Author's Conference. The selection process was based on a piece of his written work. After Corbett completed his written work and was selected to be A Young Author, he said to me, "Mom, I am so proud of myself. I have accomplished a goal that I have had since first grade." As Eleanor Roosevelt said, "You must do the thing you think you cannot do." Corbett did just that and so can you.

Another example of overcoming limitations is about my cousin Clay, who at twenty-two had an exciting life. He was working in construction building homes, racing motorcycles, hunting and fishing, enjoying each day. On the evening of June 1, 1994, Clay was driving his motorcycle through the mountains when suddenly horses galloped on to the road. Without time to stop, Clay collided into the horses causing a terrible accident. Days later he woke to devastating news. This terrible accident left him a quadriplegic. After weeks in the hospital and hours of physical therapy, Clay found life very different than before the accident. He was now confined to a wheelchair and it was a hard reality pill for a physically active young man to swallow. Most individuals would view Clay's set of circumstances as extremely difficult. Talk about limitations, but not for Clay. He accepted his limitations and they have strengthened him. To date, he continues to hunt and fish, is a professional speaker, a pro national Rockcrawler, a wheelchair athlete and a published author. Clay's personal quote is... " *push the limit, because if you never do, you will never succeed.*" He feels that his life has not really changed. "I do more now than I did before the accident. It's the best thing that ever happened to me." We could all take time to

*Chapter 3 Drive over Your Limitations*

learn a lesson or two from Clay about limitations and pushing the limit.

Learning to accept and understand limitations is only half the battle, developing strategies to accommodate limitations is the other half. Recognize the obstacles in your life that can be changed and the others that cannot and learn to manage them. Focus your attention on the qualities that you like about yourself. First, list your personal strengths or assets.

✺

✺

✺

Next, list ways you can capitalize on these strengths.

✺

✺

✺

Third, list what you believe your limitations are.

✺

✺

✺

Finally, list ways you feel you can overcome personal limitations.

✸

✸

✸

Remember to be honest and to differentiate between limitations you can and cannot manage. Often, this type of exercise can be difficult. Self evaluations can be threatening, this is not the intent. Collaborating with a friend or group of friends may help to build support and help you to work through this exercise. The goal of overcoming limitations is an essential step towards obtaining joy.

Many limitations are self-induced and are centered around circumstances involving internal factors such as fear of failing, lack of self control or denial. **Fear of failure** is the number one self induced limitation. One pays a heavy price for their fear of failing. Failure is a powerful obstacle to growth and personal fulfillment. It limits the development and progress of one's personality, preventing exploration and experimentation. We can learn from American actress Mary Pickford, "If you have made mistakes...there is another chance for you...you may have a fresh start any moment you choose, for this thing we call 'failure' is not the falling down, but the staying down." Often, there is no learning without some difficulty. If you want to keep on learning and progressing, you must risk failure.

People allow others to control their destiny because they fear they cannot. They give up before they try. The difference between success and mediocrity is accepting failure as part of life and growing from these challenges. Opera singer Beverly Sills sums it up perfectly, "You may be disappointed when you fail, but you are doomed if you don't try."

Self induced limitations come from **lack of self control**. Too often, individuals do not take control of their personal choices. If one wants to lose weight, you need to exercise and limit food intake. Sounds easy, but it's not. High fat desserts can get the best of us, why do they? What it really boils down to is a lack of self control. Personal finances are another area that is out of control for many people. The news media is constantly reporting that credit card debt is on the rise. I receive numerous calls a month from credit card companies offering me their credit card. If I did not say NO to each phone call, I would have a huge collection of credit cards.

A participant in one of my seminars told me, "Self control is no fun." My response to her was, "being out of control is less fun." Why is it less fun? Because when you're not in control of your life you can't arrange your life to feel joy. In order to feel joy you must have self control and be in control of your choices. Taking control of your weight, your attitude, and your finances requires self discipline. To be a self disciplined person requires work. A great place to start is by learning to say no to yourself. For example, **no**, I cannot spend $100.00 on a new pair of shoes this week or **no**, I will not have dessert with my dinner meal. Do not become overwhelmed with too many changes all at once. Remember the only person in this world you can control is yourself. Sooo what are you waiting for, get started!

The last self induced limitation on my list is denial or **transfer of blame.** A friend of mine worked for years in a third world country with the Peace Corps. She desired to return to the United States. When an excellent opportunity at the administrative level became available in the States, my friend applied for this position. She was very qualified for the job and felt certain she would be hired. She neglected to check on hiring details and time restrictions in reference to the position. Prior to returning to the United States to schedule an interview for this job she opted to do some traveling in Europe for two weeks. Upon arrival into the States she learned that this administrative job needed to be filled within a certain time frame and had been offered to someone else. Her reaction was to transfer blame, denying the fact that she hadn't properly checked all appropriate details concerning the hiring of this position. In other words, she blamed everyone else for her poor choice to travel for two weeks in Europe instead of jumping at the chance to interview for this new job. She was in denial of her poor choices rather than recognizing the blame was hers to own. Being accountable for your choices and accepting the consequences of those choices, positive or negative, is necessary if you desire to control internal limitations.

*Chapter 3 Drive over Your Limitations*

One of my favorite commercials is by Volkswagen that says, on the road of life there are passengers and drivers...DRIVERS WANTED. Be a driver. As the driver of your life, you determine your direction. It is a simple three step process, **evaluate, differentiate and ask**. Begin with a **self-evaluation** of your strengths and limitations. Next, **differentiate** between limitations that result from external sources and those that are self induced. The final step is the most important. **Ask** yourself, am I willing to take control of my life and begin to overcome my internal and external limitations? As you strut down your runway of life, learn to accentuate the positive and overcome the negative. Drive over your limitations and you will move closer to your established destination of feeling joy.

*Switching Lanes*

> *Let me listen to*
> *me and not to them.*
>
> —Gertrude Stein

*Switching Lanes*

## Chapter 4

# You Don't Need to Rehearse to Be Yourself

LIGHTS! CAMERA! ACTION! During my youth I spent hours rehearsing for different school and community stage productions. I loved the theater and performing in plays and musicals. I learned very quickly that a successful production required a tremendous amount of rehearsal time. I realized rehearsing lines, blocking movements on the stage, interacting with other cast members and following directions played a key role in my success as a cast member. Playing the role of a character was exciting and challenging for me. Whether it was *Fruma Sarah* in the musical, "A Fiddler on the Roof" or *Babs* in the play, "Babs Goes Dramatic," it took hours of rehearsal time to learn how to become someone else other than myself. I quickly learned that rehearsing for a play is a positive use of time, but rehearsing to be oneself is not. Have you ever felt like you had to rehearse to be yourself?

Do your family, friends or co-workers make you feel that you're on a stage rehearsing to behave the way they feel you should behave? If your answer is yes, then it's time to evaluate your relationship with those individuals. You should not have to rehearse to be yourself! Being yourself is the result of your self definition.

Listed below are three important areas that will help you to define who you are:

**1) Values**

**2) Labels**

**3) and Perceptions**

As you act out the scenes of your life, it is important to recognize that joy comes from a solid set of values. Joy is the sustained inner peace you feel when there is balance between the direction your life is moving and your self definition. When defining yourself it is essential to take a close look at your **value structure.**

A great deal of your personality and behavior is determined by your set of values. Values are behaviors and beliefs you consider worthwhile or useful. Often popular clichés such as "honesty is the best policy" or "a penny saved is a penny earned" are used to describe values. Integrity is considered a value and is defined in *The American Heritage Dictionary*, as a rigid adherence to a code of values. Integrity is a behavior that is worthwhile to most people. When integrity is lacking in one's life it becomes difficult for others to trust that person. When defining personal values, listing those qualities on paper is helpful because seeing these values on paper makes them more tangible. You will also be able to easily identify the importance of integrity in your value structure, recognizing that integrity may vary in importance in your value structure as you evaluate your relationships with family members, with each friend, with each co-worker. You are responsible for your set of values and beliefs, although many aspects of your life play a major role in molding those beliefs. It is important to recognize that you have a different value structure for each area of your life. Your value structure with family will probably differ from your value structure with friends or co-workers. **The Value Structure Chart** is an exercise designed to help you recognize and define your set of values, giving purpose and meaning to your current and future life.

## *The Value Structure Chart*

Directions: Complete the following chart as truthfully as you can. 1. In column #1 list the values that are important to you in each area of your life. 2. In column #2 give examples of when you displayed these values in your life. 3. In column #3 list how you felt about yourself when you displayed the value.

|  | #1 Value | #2 Examples of this Value | #3 My feelings |
|---|---|---|---|
| Myself: | | | |
| Family: | | | |
| Friends: | | | |
| Co-workers: | | | |

Once The Value Chart Exercise is complete, ask yourself, what does the **Value Structure Chart** reveal about obtaining and maintaining joy in my life?

Joy is felt when your definition of yourself is in balance with the direction your life is moving. The lack of joy in your life will result when this balance is jeopardized due to conflict in your value structure. At one of my seminars entitled, "Self and Stress" a woman approached me and shared her story, which illustrates this point. She told me that she and her husband were married five years prior to her becoming pregnant with their first child. She and her husband had very successful careers and seemed comfortable with the fact that she would continue to work after their baby was born. She continued to explain that as the arrival date grew closer; her husband became more uneasy with their decision. She found this irritating and frustrating. She felt that they had discussed the situation and made the decision together. It became such a problem, that they decided to seek professional help. After two months of seeing a family therapist, they discovered that her husband's uneasy feelings about her working after the birth of their child stemmed from an internal conflict with his emotional and intellectual viewpoints. His personal value structure told him that his wife should not work after the birth of their child. His mother had stayed at home to raise him and his two siblings. His religious beliefs also supported his point of view. On the other hand, his wife had a successful career and wanted to continue to work. He also had confidence that she would be able to balance both work and family effectively. With the help of their therapist, they were able to work through this conflict. Today, the wife continues to work outside their home. They have had another child and all is going well for their family. For some, professional therapy can be the key to resolving conflict that results from imbalance in a value structure.

**Labels** are a classification which plays a key role in establishing your self definition. Think back to your early formative years of childhood. Can you remember being labeled according to lack of or abundance of talents or special abilities? It is those labels that influenced the development of your personal definition. For example, while my two sisters and I all have artistic talent and abilities, my sister, Cathy, was labeled the artist. Cathy spent her time in school taking several art related courses and developed her talent beyond that of Debra's and mine. While growing up we were continually reminded of Cathy's incredible art talent and ability. Cathy received recognition and accolades for her artistic creations. Debra and I were content and comfortable with the fact that Cathy was the Artist in our family. Years later, Debra and I have come to recognize that we also have artistic talent to be valued. Debra has found pottery and designing silver jewelry to be her artistic outlet. It was not until I moved away from home and was hired as an artist for a publishing company that I began to recognize and develop my own artistic flair.

Labels, when used as a positive reinforcement of abilities, can motivate. However, when used in a negative connotation, labels can be detrimental to one's self-esteem, causing inner conflict. When you find yourself feeling inner conflict and it becomes difficult to pinpoint the source, take a close look at the labels that comprise your self definition. It is positive and healthy to make adjustments. Getting to know yourself and understanding labels that describe you will allow you the freedom to feel comfortable with making change in personal labels, then moving closer to feeling inner peace and joy.

## Chapter 4 You Don't Need to Rehearse to Be Yourself

**Perceptions** are insights you feel towards yourself. They are essential in assessing your feelings about yourself. The perceptions that you feel about yourself come from both internal and external sources. The internal source is yourself and those feelings you have about yourself. The external source comes from other people in your life and how you believe they feel about you. When you feel conflict between your personal feelings regarding yourself and the outside information sent by others, your self-worth suffers. The result of this conflict is that you begin to feel decreased joy in your life. You will need to take the challenge and respond positively to making change in your life. It is your decision to accept or reject this external information. People resist change because of their fear to fail. Do not allow others to dictate what you do or how you act because you fear change.

You must resolve conflict between internal and external sources of information in order to feel joy. It is up to you to understand your value structure, shed yourself of negative labels and embrace the opportunity to change values, labels and perceptions. Do not feel that you need to rehearse to be yourself. Life is not a staged play with a script that is written by others for you to memorize and act out. Do not allow your associates to make you feel that you are on a stage rehearsing lines to behave the way they feel you should behave. Be yourself and feel comfortable living your life according to your self definition. **You don't need to** *rehearse* **to be yourself.**

Switching Lanes

> *Success is often achieved by those who don't know failure is inevitable.*
> —Coco Chanel

*Switching Lanes*

Chapter 5

# The Game of Life

The Milton Bradley board game LIFE challenges participants to test their negotiating skills with real life situations. The players move car shaped game pieces across a board challenging their skill. Unlike real life they spin a number wheel, collect money and LIFE tiles while attending college, changing careers and reaping the rewards of retirement resulting in big dividends or bankruptcy. The end results in the game are exciting with harmless pretend consequences. However, choices made in life require careful consideration and planning. Success is a journey based on skilled strategy, proceeding forward one move at a time, not a destination.

For some people, the journey is more important than the destination, achieving success lasts a lifetime. How you define success determines what challenges or risks in life you are willing to take. According to *Webster's* dictionary success is defined as: 1) The achievement of something desired or attempted. 2) The gaining of fame or prosperity. In order to find balance in your life, it is important to establish your personal definition of success.

Trying to coordinate your life's activities and schedules to meet all personal obligations can become quite a juggling act. An important step towards scheduling your personal time is to prioritize activities and appointments by importance and urgency. You should see a pattern developing, that is helping you to recognize what priority your family and friends have in your schedule. Scheduling time with the people you love and care about will help you achieve personal balance in your life. This will also help you resolve feelings of guilt that result from the lack of time spent with family and friends. Create a schedule that you can easily commit to by prioritizing and simplifying your time.

An important concept to recognize and understand is that you are in control of determining your worth. Do not allow material objects or money to define your worth. You can follow the lead of Mary McCarthy, an American novelist and critic, who said, "We are the heroes of our own story." Too often I hear people comment on another's success based on material objects such as the car they drive or the house they purchased. If you think you are of little worth, others will too. If you feel positive about yourself others will also. You can realize your self worth by the contributions you share with others such as your time and talents not the material objects you possess. You can work on being the hero of your own story by taking an inventory of yourself.

Complete the following **Self Inventory Exercise**. It is designed to be quick and simple in helping you to clarify the parts of yourself that need simple adjustments, while recognizing your personal traits that do not need change. You should not be surprised if when you focus on family, friends and colleagues, outcomes will vary. For instance, you may note that procrastination is a problem for you in your home environment but not in the workplace. You need to understand that different talents and skills are required in different environments. After completing the exercise you will recognize traits about yourself that need to be altered and other traits about yourself that do not need change. The important factor is to realize that you are in charge of yourself and defining your self worth.

## *Self Inventory Exercise*

**Directions:** Complete each statement below. The results will help you determine your personal traits and what simple adjustments are needed in your lifestyle.

**I. At Home with family members**

A. Personal traits that I value in myself....

   1.

   2.

B. Personal traits about myself that I would like to change...

   1.

2.

C. I will change the following trait(s) about myself by….

1.

2.

## II. With my colleagues

A. Personal traits that I value in myself…

1.

2.

B. Personal traits about myself that I would like to change…

1.

2.

C. I will change the following trait(s) about myself by…

1.

2.

**III. With Friends**

A. Personal traits that I value in myself…

1.

2.

B. Personal traits about myself that I would like to change…

1.

2.

C. I will change the following trait(s) about myself by…

1.

2.

Now that you have completed the **Self Inventory Exercise** highlight the helpful information concerning your personal traits. A given trait you exemplify may be a strength in your work environment and a source of conflict at home. For example, at work your ability to take charge of a situation and delegate tasks to co-workers may be a positive trait; however in your family environment that trait may cause frustration amongst family members. This exercise is designed to help you assess your personal traits and skills in various environments allowing you to start recognizing when the trait is appropriate and when it is not. Using a trait inappropriately may diminish your self worth based on the negative feedback from others.

If you find your work environment and job responsibilities overwhelming you need to determine the reason. Do you have the ability to make changes in your work environment? If so, make the necessary adjustments to stream-line and organize your work space, making you more efficient. Are you using your time effectively? Everyone has the same twenty four hours in a day, therefore what we don't use we lose. Ask yourself, if time were money how would I be spending mine? Time is a valuable commodity and most people do not feel that they have enough of it. Some individuals use their time more skillfully than others. Arrange your day with the highest priority tasks topping your to do list. Stay focused on the task at hand completing one task and then move to the next. The multi-task approach is not always the best. Organize yourself and you will find that your job becomes less overwhelming. Living in today's world creates the constant challenge of making good use of one's time.

Your approach to time management and how wisely you use it changes over the years. When you're young, you think you have all the time in the world. However, as you get older you begin to recognize how fast time is running out. It is at this point that panic sets in and you begin to feel anxiety over the fact that you don't have enough time to do all you need to do. To relieve some of your time related anxiety you need to take control of your life and your time. Do not over extend yourself by planning too much for one day. This only creates frustration and a feeling of failure.

When planning your daily schedule be realistic about your time.

Another way to take control of your time is to organize your life. Overhaul a small portion of your life and then another. Too much change all at once can create anxiety. Remember the importance of delegating. Communicate with family members, friends and co-workers your need for assistance with certain tasks. You are only one person, many hands make the work load light and working as a team is a valuable concept.

You should take a close look at your goals, both setting them and achieving them. Goals are only obtainable if they are realistic. Goal setting is an effective way to focus on a given area of your life that you desire to improve. Changing behavior requires a great deal of self control and self discipline. Your success at setting and achieving goals will be determined by your desire to change behavior.

Goal setting can be highly effective if approached correctly. To set a goal is the first step; to accomplish the goal is the challenge. When you approach goal setting, take it one step at a time. Start with something small, make a plan, feel success and then move on to another goal.

After setting the goal write it on paper and place it in a visible spot, perhaps on your refrigerator or bathroom mirror. A goal written down and reviewed daily is more likely to be accomplished. You control the goal setting process in your life. Be kind to yourself and not overly critical when setting and accomplishing goals. If you experience a set back, you should take time out to re-evaluate your goal and the plan. It may be necessary to make adjustments. Don't look at this as a failure. The key is to set realistic goals and then back it up with an effective plan of action.

The challenge of keeping your life in balance is an on-going process. Begin to move towards joy in your life by taking control of your time. Prioritize and simplify your daily calendar. Include time for family and friends in your schedule. Your joy and self worth are controlled by you. Finally, set realistic goals for yourself with a manageable plan of action. American poet, Emily Dickinson said, "The mere sense of living is joy enough." So when you begin to recognize success as a journey and not a destination you'll discover yourself traveling along the road to finding joy. You must arrange your life so joy is likely and success is the reward. The following poem, by an unknown author, expresses how joy is a state of mind.

> *Learn to count your garden by the flowers,*
> *Never by the leaves that fall.*
> *Count your days by the golden hours;*
> *Don't remember clouds at all.*
> *Count your nights by stars, not by shadows.*
> *Count your years with smiles not tears.*
> *Count your blessings, not your troubles.*
> *Count your age by friends, not years.*

> Kind words can be short
> and easy to speak, but their
> echoes are truly endless.
>
> —Mother Teresa

*Switching Lanes*

## Chapter 6

# Recharge Your Life

Have you ever been frustrated by a dead car battery? Nothing is more aggravating than getting into your car and turning the key only to realize that your car battery is dead. The solution to remedy the situation is quite simple, to have the battery recharged. This is true with yourself as well. If you begin feeling like your motor is running in low gear due to the stress in your life, your hectic schedule or the daily demands from your family or job, it is time to have your personal battery recharged.

Learning to recharge your life will require change. Your personal battery is probably low because you are on overload. You know yourself better than anyone else, therefore, only you will be able to recharge your life. Why not try this simple seven step plan I have developed?

**1) Selective Hearing** is the first step towards setting your own internal standard and establishing an action plan to recharge your battery. In chapter #1 the Sticky Note Theory was introduced, illustrating that you receive daily verbal and non verbal messages from other people. Some of these messages are positive and others negative. The way you process that information is up to you. Positive messages uplift and esteem you while negative messages can minimize your self worth. You cannot control the messages that are sent your way, but you can reject negative information that you receive from others. Learn to value selective hearing and how to implement it. Your ability to process incoming information from others will increase your ability to recharge yourself.

**2) Listen to your inner voice.** Many people refer to their inner-self as a gut-level feeling or their sixth sense. The reference word isn't what's important, what is important is your ability to listen. How many times have you tuned out inner feelings and later regretted doing so? The sudden urge to pick up the telephone to call a friend or the feeling that a right turn is better than a left when driving to a new location are examples of the inner voice. You should become acquainted with your inner voice, trust your instincts, and then listen.

I learned the value of my inner voice in high school and later in my life. In school I had a difficult time with academic testing. I was frequently told to always trust my instincts and not second guess myself while taking tests. As a sophomore in high school, my English teacher taught me to go with my first answer and not the second or third. Applying this concept proved to be very positive for me and resulted in higher test scores and academic grades.

A decade later this concept was reinforced again in my life by my business partner, Debbi. The importance of listening to our inner voices while working with business clients gave us the insight and confidence to introduce new and innovative fashion show options to our clients, like using live afghan dogs as show props. In business applying this concept proved to be the creative edge we needed to set our business apart from many other fashion show production companies. Listening to my inner voice has proven to be very effective for me in my personal and professional life. Today, I continue to apply this valuable information in all areas of my life.

Try not to second guess yourself. Doubting yourself may result in insecure feelings and a sense of confusion or lack of self control. In order to increase your self confidence it is essential to know who you are and to listen to your inner voice. You will find the results of this behavior positive and energizing.

**3) Take the high road** by adjusting your attitude. Are you spending too much time looking at the glass half empty instead of half full? The way you view situations and problems will impact your attitude. If your attitude needs adjusting begin by asking yourself, how can I get from where I am to where I want to be? If you think negatively, you will see negative in your life. If you think positively, you will see situations in a positive way. In other words, you are what you think.

To begin, establish a plan to help chart your attitude course. My husband, Jeff, was a navigator in the U.S. Air Force when we were first married. It was his job to chart the course the plane would fly to get from destination A to destination B. The map he used to chart the course was called a flight plan. He would spend hours drafting a flight plan prior to departure time. If Jeff failed to provide a well diagramed, accurate flight plan this would prevent the entire crew from being able to execute an effective scheduled mission. An important component in formulating your personal life's course is your attitude. Your attitude is your state of mind and feelings. One should establish an accurate plan in an effort to adjust your attitude and always remember to take the high road as you travel through life.

**4) Serve yourself a daily dose of gratitude.** Giving thanks is an ancient virtue and has been done by generations of people before us. The Pilgrims are a perfect example. We celebrate Thanksgiving each year because of their celebration of thanks centuries ago at Plymouth. Today, hectic lifestyles prevent people from recognizing their blessings. Expressing gratitude for one's blessings will lift your spirits and focus your mood in a positive direction. Feeling positive will boost your energy and recharge your life. Take time daily to give thanks to yourself, others and God for those gifts that bless your life.

**5) Shine the spotlight on you and others.** It is essential that you take time to shine the spotlight on yourself each day. There is nothing wrong with wanting to

*Chapter 6 Recharge Your Life*

be the best you. In fact, you must take time from your hectic daily schedule to give time to yourself. Do something each day you enjoy. In the beginning this may be difficult, taking time for yourself. Begin with five minutes a day and then as that becomes a part of your routine gradually increase the time. For some, a simple act of kindness for themself might be to set aside time for a bubble bath or lunch with a friend. Others may prefer to read a book or to take a brisk walk. This is not being selfish; this act of kindness for yourself, is healthy.

Another positive way to recharge yourself is to shine the spotlight on those around you. Lose yourself in service and soon your personal problems won't seem so overwhelming. Take the time to call a friend or mail a 'cheery' note to a family member. You will quickly discover that you feel energized and revitalized by spending your time doing simple acts of kindness for others. Mother Teresa, an Albanian missionary said it best, "Let no one ever come to you without leaving better and happier. Be the living expression of God's kindness; kindness in your face, kindness in your eyes, kindness in your smile."

**6) Simplify your life.** This process of simplifying one's life can be difficult but it is necessary. Refer back to Chapter One and review The Joy Circle Questionnaire. Adjustments to your Joy Circle will enable you to simplify your life one step at a time. Finding joy in your life comes when your joy circle is in balance. In order to achieve that balance you may need to remove those activities, associations and assets that drain your energy. Ask yourself, what postpones joy in my life? Your answer will most likely involve stress. A common stress for many people is imbalance in their life due to being over-scheduled.

**7) Enjoy your successes.** Learn to embrace and appreciate your accomplishments. American Poet, Waldo Emerson said, "Scatter joy". That is great advice to follow and to incorporate into your life. In today's world it is important to help others and to give of yourself and your time. It is okay to acknowledge that your contributions are of value. Allow your behavior and expectations to be based on what YOU genuinely want for yourself, not what others want for you. Feel satisfaction with today. Move on by taking time for yourself and making service a part of your routine. If you focus on the negative and the unhappiness in your life then that is what you will become. If you focus on the positive in your life then that is what you will become.

Recharging your life is your responsibility. You may find this simple seven step plan an effective approach to use, relying on all seven steps or a combination of a few. If you need additional support with this process reference magazine articles or seek out professional guidance. The important thing to focus on is that you can recharge your life and move towards a better you.

> *I hoped the trip would be
> the best of all journeys:
> a journey into ourselves.*
> —Shirley MacLaine

*Switching Lanes*

## Chapter 7

# Switching Lanes

Have you ever been driving down the road and because of construction or a traffic accident you are forced to switch lanes? This can cause feelings of frustration and aggravation. Due to an accident or construction, traffic patterns are altered forcing the speed of traffic to slow down. As a motorist, one does not anticipate or choose the changes in traffic patterns but becomes involved in the change because of the decision to drive a certain road or highway. The road my life was traveling a few years ago was fairly smooth with limited bumps or traffic jams. Suddenly the road blocks began and I have had the opportunity to tap deep in to my personal feelings. My first speaking partner, Sherry, passed away from a sudden heart attack, my father's struggle with Parkinson's disease has become more difficult, and just this past year my sister Cathy was diagnosed with cancer. These events forced me to switch lanes. I did not choose these alterations in my life but I accept them and am finding ways to proceed forward, but with caution I must add. This road I now travel is new for me and I am at times uncertain about the direction I am moving.

As I reflect over the chapters of this book I recognize that each one of us must put its content to the test. Each of us must strive to **balance** our days and continue to find the time to **recharge our lives** and **not postpone joy.**

Provided in this book are tools to assist you in the process of balancing your life; The Joy Circle, The Self Inventory Exercise, The Value Structure Chart, and The Action Plan for Joy. As you travel down the road of life allow these tools to help you move towards securing inner peace and joy in your life.

I am grateful for the opportunity I had to learn many wonderful lessons from Sherry and to have grown in friendship with her. Daily, I marvel at my Dad's ability to be positive about his life as Parkinson's disease robs him of his mobility and memory. His sense of humor continues to brighten my days, reminding me that laughter is contagious and uplifting. I give thanks to God that my sister, Cathy, has survived cancer and is finding the inner strength emotionally and physically to fight her battle.

Don't allow others to trespass on your joy. Your sense of self worth must come from within, not from outside sources. You have the right to your feelings. Learn to express them in a positive way and allow others to express theirs. Avoid shutting down your emotional side; it helps to give balance to the total you. Expressing emotions is healthy.

A key to personal growth is to know your feelings, attitudes and emotions. Understanding emotions gives you a new perspective about yourself and others. Therefore, you can promote your ability to define new perspectives, inner growth and self awareness. Inner growth needs to happen before development of outward strengths surface.

The French writer Collett said, "What a wonderful life I've had...I only wish I'd realized it sooner." Don't wait until tragedy enters your life to realize the value of each day. Learn to recognize you have the ability and responsibility to control your own life. You have the right to be treated with respect and to be taken seriously. You have the ability to say **no**, without feeling guilty. You are entitled to feel joy. I appreciate the opportunity I've had to switch lanes in life and to recognize joy in my journey regardless of how bumpy the road.

**Recognize that you have a wonderful life and remember...don't postpone joy.**

> *Love yourself first and
> everything else falls
> into line. You really have to
> love yourself to get anything
> done in this world.*
>
> —Lucille Ball

www.ingramcontent.com/pod-product-compliance
Lightning Source LLC
Chambersburg PA
CBHW071730040426
42446CB00011B/2297